Our Rights

How Kids are Changing the World

written and illustrated by Janet Wilson

Second Story Press

United Nations Convention on the Rights of the Child

Article 1: Everyone under 18 is equal and has the same rights.

Article 2: You shall be protected against all forms of discrimination. No child shall be treated unfairly.

Article 3: Your best interest must be put first in all decisions affecting you.

Article 4: The government is responsible for protecting your rights.

Article 5: Your family is to create an environment where you can reach your potential.

Article 6: You have the right to be alive.

Article 7: You have the right to a name and a nationality.

Article 8: You have the right to know and be cared for by your parents.

Article 9-11: You should not be separated from your parents unless it is harmful. You have the right to stay in contact with them.

Article 12: You have the right to express your opinions and to have them respected and considered in all matters concerning you.

Article 13: You should have access to information. You can say or express what you think unless it harms others.

Article 14: You have the freedom to choose a religion.

Article 15: You can choose your own friends and join groups and organizations.

Article 16: You have the right to privacy.

Article 17: You should be protected from harmful material.

Article 18: Both your parents are responsible for your upbringing and development.

Article 19: If you suffer abuse, neglect, or exploitation, you have the right to help and support services.

Article 20 & 21: You have the right to special care if you can't live with your family, or if you are adopted or in foster care.

Article 22: Refugee children have the right to help and protection, and to reunite with families, if possible.

Article 23: Disabled children have the right to special care and education to live a full life.

Article 24-25: You have the right to health care, safe water, nutritious food, and a clean environment. If in care, your situation should be periodically reviewed.

Article 26-27: You have the right to social security and adequate living conditions.

Article 28-29: You have the right to a good primary education that develops respectful values and prepares you for a responsible adult life.

Article 30: Minority or indigenous children have the right to their own culture, language, and religion.

Article 31: You have the right to relax and play, and join in cultural and artistic activities.

Article 32-33: You have the right to protection against harmful or hazardous work and illegal drugs.

Article 34: You have the right to help and protection from sexual exploitation including prostitution and pornographic materials.

Article 35-37: No one can kidnap, sell, or cruelly punish or harm you.

Article 38: Children under 16 never have to join armies. Children in war zones should receive special protection.

Article 39: Victims of exploitation, torture, or armed conflicts have the right to receive help to restore their self-respect.

Article 40: Children accused of crimes have the right to be treated fairly and with dignity.

Article 41: If the laws of a country protect children better than the articles in this Convention, those laws should stay.

Article 42: All children and adults should be informed of the rights in the Convention.

Adapted from the United Nations Convention of the Rights of the Child.
www2.ohchr.org/english/law/crc.htm

The Star Thrower

When the first pearl light of dawn appeared on the horizon, a man set out for his daily walk along the ocean shore.

What a shame! he thought, noticing all the starfish that had washed far onto the beach in the storm the night before. *The poor creatures will surely die when the sun rises.*

Then the man's attention was drawn to a girl in the distance, bending, stretching, and waving her arms. *Perhaps she is dancing to welcome the new day*, he thought. He smiled remembering the energy and joy of youth. As he neared, the man realized the girl was throwing starfish into the sea.

"My dear, there are more starfish stranded on this beach than you can possibly save. Surely you cannot hope to make a difference."

The girl tossed another starfish gently into the ocean.

"I made a difference to that one."

"When I first realized that I could make a change in the world, my skin tingled with excitement. It still does." **Craig Kielburger**, Canada, founded Free The Children when he was 12 after learning that Iqbal Masih, a carpet worker in Pakistan of the same age, was murdered for exposing the cruelty of child slavery.

"We are the world's children." **Gabriela Arrieta**, 13, Bolivia, was the first child to speak to the world's leaders at the United Nations World Summit for Children, 2002. Young people from 154 countries discussed ways to make a difference. This is an excerpt from their report, *A World Fit For Us:*

"We are the victims of exploitation and abuse. We are street children. We are the children of war. We are the victims and orphans of HIV/AIDS. We are denied good-quality education and health care. We are victims of political, economic, cultural, religious, and environmental discrimination. We are children whose voices are not being heard: it is time we are taken into account. We want a world fit for children, because a world fit for us is a world fit for everyone. You call us the future, but we are also the present. We are not the sources of problems; we are the resources that are needed to solve them. We are not expenses; we are investments. We are not just young people; we are people and citizens of this world."
www.unicef.org/worldfitforchildren

The star thrower is one of a galaxy of bright stars—children who are part of a powerful and growing force daring to create a better world by standing up and speaking out for their right to be treated equally, to live in dignity, and to have their opinions respected.

In 1989, the United Nations' *Convention on the Rights of the Child* declared that all children have basic human rights, regardless of race, sex, religion, or any other status. They also needed to be informed of their rights. Promises were made to children that these rights would be honored; yet the majority of children still live in poverty, go to bed hungry, and are denied education. Millions are victims of violence, war, exploitation, and abuse. Girls are especially vulnerable. One child in five dies from preventable causes.

Children want the Convention promises to be kept. They understand that rights come with responsibilities. Like our star thrower, they are taking responsibility to help defend the rights of children—one star at a time.

Dylan Mahalingam, 11, USA

"Our success in the collective power of youth using the Internet assures me that age will never be an impediment to making a difference."

Dylan speaks about using the Internet to mobilize kids to take action.

"'Don't waste your food, Dylan! Some families live for a week on what you are wasting,' my parents used to say when I didn't want to finish my vegetables. Even at the age of 3, I wondered how I could get those veggies onto the plate of others who needed them. I first witnessed the realities of poverty on a family trip to India when I was 8. I saw parents struggling to feed their kids. I saw young girls working in a brickyard. I learned that many children die from diseases because they cannot afford a vaccine that costs less than 25 cents. I felt angry, sad, and helpless. I felt guilty for wasting food. In 2004, after the devastating earthquake and tsunami, I gathered a group of kids from different schools to build a website to raise funds. To my surprise, kids over the world came together to raise more than $700,000. This inspired me to co-found Lil' MDGs to use the Internet, digital, and social media to empower children in all corners of the world. The name is derived from the United Nations' Millennium Development Goals (MDGs)—the pledge made in 2000 by 189 countries to cut global poverty in half by 2015. Since then we have mobilized more than four million children worldwide from 41 countries. I never imagined that my parents' nagging about wasting food and our trip would be such transforming experiences for me."

Dylan says:
Every child has the right to live; unfortunately, every child does not have an equal chance of survival.

The goals of the MDGs are to: #1 eradicate extreme hunger and poverty; #2 achieve universal primary education; #3 empower girls and women and treat both genders equally; #4 reduce child mortality; #5 improve maternal health; #6 halt and reverse the spread of HIV/AIDS and other major diseases; #7 ensure clean drinking water and a toilet; #8 develop a strong global partnership between poor and rich countries.

Eight Millennium Goals—a reverse poem to be read forward and backward.

There is no way to achieve the eight millennium goals/ I do not believe that/ People can be peaceful and work together/ Why doesn't everyone think/ Diseases like AIDS aren't that important to get rid of/ It's a lie that/ Children need to be educated/ I don't understand why people don't believe/ No one should be free/ Who would think that/ Everyone is created equal.
—by **Lacey**

Anita Khushwaha, 15, India

"Girls are free to fly like honey bees
and make their lives as sweet as honey."

Anita learned not to fear the bees.

Girls born into lower caste societies in India are expected to spend their lives shepherding goats, marrying young, and having many children—but this was not for Anita Khushwaha. When she was 6, Anita wanted to go to school so desperately she persuaded her parents to allow her to attend. Anita earned money for school fees by teaching other children and running errands for beekeepers. At 15, she boldly refused to be married. She pretended to go on a hunger strike for four days until her parents gave in. Anita had a dream—to become a beekeeper. But making honey was considered dangerous work, suitable for males only. Anita was not afraid of bees. She saved money for a year to buy a bee box with one queen bee. When the box began yielding honey, she bought a second one. Everyone called Anita crazy. They laughed when she was stung. But when her business started making a profit, people stopped teasing her. Now they called her "the Queen Bee." Within four years, Anita had more than one hundred boxes. She bought a bike and enrolled in college. Her success inspired other families to take up beekeeping. Anita was named a UNICEF poster girl for helping to eliminate gender bias and becoming an inspiring role model for millions of girls in India. Now, every girl in Anita's village attends school.

Anita says:

A dream doesn't become reality through magic; it takes sweat, determination, and hard work.

Education breaks the cycle of poverty, especially for girls. One out of six children in the world does not attend school. Millions of others receive little or substandard instruction. Many countries deny children of ethnic minorities and girls an adequate education. School fees or the cost of uniforms keep many poor children out of school, dramatically limiting their future. Girls are subject to gender-based infanticide, malnutrition, and neglect. Ninety per cent of child domestic workers are girls.

When **Thandiwe Chama**, 8, learned her school in Zambia closed because there were no teachers, she led a walk with sixty children in search of another school.

"At 7 boys go to school. At 7 girls clean the house. At 12 boys play sports. At 12 girls get married. At 14 boys are still playing. At 14 girls are having babies."—**Peggy**, 17, Kenya

"If you want positive change, it must start within yourself."

Emanuel works with kids in Manila's slums.

"Love learning and it will love you back and enable you to change your world." Emanuel listened intently to the guest speaker at his grade eight graduation. Em, as he liked to be called, wanted an education, but he was ridiculed by other kids who quit school and joined gangs. After being bullied and beaten, Em felt he had no choice but to become a gang member. The speaker had been tempted to quit school, too, but instead he decided to fight the bullies by getting an education. He also talked about his shame of growing up poor in the slums and scavenging in the garbage piles. Em lived in poverty, too. He had been rising at 3 a.m. to wash trucks and find things in the dump to sell since he was 9. On weekends, he sold corn from a cart to earn money to be able to go to school. After the ceremony, Em met the man, Harnin Manalaysay, who would change the course of his life. Em was inspired to join his Club 8586 and later, the Dynamic Teen Company, a group that works in the slums to provide poor children with food and basic medical care to keep them from joining gangs, taking drugs, or committing petty crimes. Em used his pushcart to bring books and school supplies to teach kids basic education and founded Mind Your Rights (M.Y. Rights) to reduce the cycle of abuse and neglect of children by teaching parents, educators, and children their basic rights. Em also created a coloring book, *A Child's Rights*, that has been used in schools.

Emanuel says:

Kids on the streets are victims. They need understanding more than money, love more than bread. Let's not waste our time judging them. Let's take the challenge to help them.

One in six of the world's 5 to 14-year-olds—an estimated 158 million—is engaged in child labor. Their work in mines, with chemicals and pesticides in agriculture, or with machinery in factories is often dangerous. Millions of girls who work as domestic servants are especially vulnerable to exploitation and abuse. Education is the key to preventing child labor. Also, alternative sources of income need to be developed so that families won't have to depend on a child's earnings.

"We, the world's children, are wearing white bands to make poverty history. We need more than promises—we need actions. Poverty is manmade and man can undo it." **Message from C8 youth at the G8 conference**, UK, 2005

Shannen Koostachin, 13, Canada

"In Aboriginal principle, the circle has no beginning, no end; no one is in front, behind, above, or below. Together we keep the circle strong."

Shannen spoke on the steps of the Canadian Parliament in 2008.

"School is a time for hopes and dreams of the future. We want the same hope as every other Canadian student." Shannen trembled as she faced hundreds of demonstrators on the lawn of the Canadian Parliament. The presence of her friends, family, and elders gave her courage to continue speaking. She described the conditions of the run-down portables in her remote northern reserve of Attawapiskat First Nation. "I want to tell you what it is like to never feel excited about being educated. It's hard to feel pride when your classrooms are cold. It's hard to feel you can have the chance to grow up to be somebody important when you don't have proper resources like libraries." After Shannen's school was polluted with diesel oil, the government brought in temporary portables. After the third promise to build a new school was broken, Shannen's eighth grade class gave up their grad trip to go to Ottawa to challenge the government. "Today I am sad because the Indian Affairs minister told me that there was no money to build a new school. I don't believe him! When I shook his hand, I told him that the children won't quit." Shannen made a video encouraging students to write letters to the government asking for the same rights and funding for all First Nations children. This largest youth-driven, children's rights movement in Canadian history moved the government to finally keep its promise, but Shannen will never see her new school. She died in a car accident at 15. Her dream lives on.

Shannen said:

Don't be afraid to follow your dreams. Never give up hope. Stand up and speak for what you believe in.

Indigenous children face discrimination and violation of their rights. Compared to non-native children, they have higher rates of school dropout, substance addictions, and death due to illness and suicide. Poverty forces more children into care and the juvenile justice system. First Nations around the world are greatly affected by pollution and climate change.

"I don't know what they find so scary about me. I just want them to hear what I have to say."

Sliammon activist, **Ta'Kaiya Blaney**, 10, sang her song, Shallow Waters, outside the offices of a company proposing an oil pipeline from the Alberta tar sands to Canada's northwest coast after they turned her away. She co-wrote the song to raise awareness of the devastation a supertanker oil spill would cause to marine and coastal life, and the traditional First Nations way of life.

Zach Bonner, 12, USA

"I feel it's important for everyone to have the opportunity to just be a kid."

Zach, at at the age of 6, collected water for the homeless.

Some kids love to skateboard or play baseball or video games. Zach Bonner loves to volunteer. When he was 6, Zach took his red wagon door-to-door to collect water for families left homeless by a hurricane. After receiving enough donations to fill 27 truckloads, Zach established the Little Red Wagon Foundation to aid more than one million homeless children in the USA. He supplied "Zachpacks" filled with donated snacks, toys, and toiletries to children living in shelters or displaced by natural disasters. He organized an event that simulated being homeless for 24 hours. As Zach became more aware of the difficulties facing homeless youth, he raised awareness and funds with a walk of more than 1,000 miles (1,600 km) from Tampa, Florida, to Washington, DC. He called it My House to the White House. His mother and a friend drove behind in a donated van with a red wagon on the top. When Zach got discouraged or bored and felt like quitting, he thought about the homeless kids. "They don't have a safe place to sleep at night. They're out on the streets not because they want to be, but because it's out of their control." Since then, Zach has walked to the Pacific coast, 2,478 miles (3,988 km) in total. He says, "This is what I enjoy doing."

Zach says:

When you combine the wisdom and experience of an adult with the spirit of a kid, great things will happen.

"I need to study hard and save a lot of money." **Deepak Prahlad**, 10, India, is a rag picker who dreams of being a doctor. He saves his earnings in a special bank created and run by street children for street children where they can safely store their money.

Approximately 150 million children live or work on the streets. Most suffer from malnutrition, hunger, health problems, and abuse. They have to work several jobs or steal to survive. Street children deserve respect as valuable members of society. Some run businesses to support their families and friends. They have the right to education, health and safety services, and counselling to help them move off the street.

"We street children are by ourselves; we have no one in front or behind who cares for us. There is no one to cry for us when we die." **Rewat Timilshina**, Nepal.

Nujood Ali, 10, Yemen

"I hated the night. I cried so much, but no one listened to me."

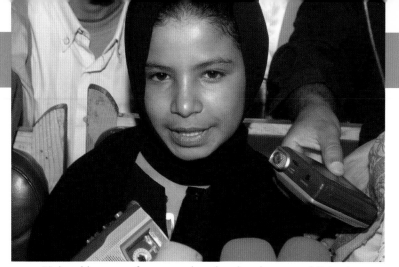

Nujood became famous when her book was published.

Nujood Ali sank into the back of the bench, bewildered and alone. People scarcely noticed her, or if they did, they probably wondered why she was not in school. Nujood had never been inside a courthouse, but had seen one on television and knew people went there for help. As the crowds cleared, a judge noticed the little girl dressed in black. "I want a divorce," Nujood whispered to him, "and I want to go back to school." Two months before, Nujood's parents had taken her out of the second grade to marry a man three times her age, an ancient custom still practiced in her traditional community. Nujood had no idea what a marriage was. She was a simple village girl who always said yes to the orders of her father and brothers. Today, she was saying no. When her husband had allowed Nujood to visit her parents that day, she found a way to escape by taking a bus to the courthouse in the city. She told the judge, "My husband beat me and did bad things to me. I would run from one room to another, but he would catch me." Nujood was granted her divorce. Inspired by her bravery, other girls came forward to sue for divorce. Nujood has co-written a book, *I am Nujood, Age 10 and Divorced*. She wants to become a lawyer to help other girls in Yemen, where more than half are married before they're 18.

Nujood says:
No one has the right to keep me from justice.

Girls from poor families are married off to virtual strangers before puberty to provide for their future. Child marriage is a vicious circle—girls drop out of school and bear too many children, contributing to high female illiteracy and birth rates. Pregnancy and childbirth is the leading cause of death in teens in the developing world.

"Apart from the health hazards, the ancient tradition of female circumcision leads to early marriage and motherhood which brings an end to schooling and leads to other missed opportunities."

Teresa Cheptoo, 13, Kenya, works tirelessly to teach girls and boys the negative health, psychological, and social consequences of the harmful practice of Female Genital Mutilation (FMG).

"I'm a school child. What am I meant to do among all these weapons?"

Ndale says his life has begun again since he escaped.

"I was 11 years old. It was an ordinary day. I woke up at sunrise, washed, put on my school uniform, and walked to school with six classmates. Suddenly, two armed soldiers kidnapped us. We walked for three days without eating or sleeping or talking. They kicked us if we walked too slowly. It was like a nightmare, but it was real. When we reached the camp, our school uniforms were burned and we were given soldiers' uniforms. 'This is your pen now,' one soldier said, passing me a rifle. Once we knew how to handle our weapons, they said it was time to learn to kill people. One day we were attacked by another army taking revenge for our men stealing a cow. We children had to go first. Someone began to shoot. People were falling down dead beside me. People were screaming. I can't describe how scared I was. When I tried to hide, soldiers shoved me forward and said, 'If your friend dies, it doesn't matter. Just step over him!' Two of my school friends were killed on the very first day. The fighting continued for 12 days. All that over a cow." Three years later, after Ndale managed to flee, he returned to school. As a representative of child soldiers, Ndale sat on the jury to nominate candidates for the World's Children's Prize for the Rights of the Child. Each year millions of children from around the world hold a global vote to choose a winner.

Ndale says:

All adults must remember that they have been children. Many adults forget that.

"Children should not be used as pawns in wars that adults choose to fight. The enormous money spent on futile wars could be diverted into education, poverty reduction, and job training for neglected youths to alleviate the conditions that fuel wars." **Salifu Kamara**, 15, Sierra Leone. Believing that even a child can change the world through peace, Salifu is an advocate for the rights of other physically disabled and emotionally traumatized child soldiers.

On February 12, former child soldiers and youth from around the world present symbolic "red hands" to their leaders to demand stronger action to end the use of child soldiers. The Convention on the Rights of the Child prohibits the forced recruitment or use of children under the age of 16 in armed conflict, but child soldiers are still being used in more than a dozen countries. It is estimated that one in ten soldiers in the world is a child.

Mayra Avellar Neves, 15, Brazil

"We can and must stand up for children,
whose rights are being violated and whose lives are at risk."

Mayra receives 2008 Children's Peace prize from Archbishop Tutu.

"My name is Mayra Avellar Neves. Can you imagine how it is to live your life with a war going on in front of your door? Is it fair that we have to wake up with the sound of bullets? I live in one of the poorest *favelas* [slums] in Rio de Janeiro. For years the drug cartels have waged wars with each other and with the police. People have become accustomed to the violence that claims thousands of lives each year. It is often impossible to go out into the street because it's too dangerous. One boy in the street emptied the trash and he was shot in his head by the police who mistook him for a criminal because he was black. When I was 11, the violence was so extreme that schools and clinics were closed. All children should have a safe upbringing and the right to an education. Without an education they are at risk of being recruited by the drug gangs. Many children in the favelas believe it is their destiny to live in poverty and violence. I refuse to accept this. I want to tell people that even though they don't have money, they can stand up for their rights."

Mayra Avellar organized peace marches to ask the police to use less violence and stop patrolling near the school. She helped make a documentary, *Cruzeiro*. Since then, life in the favelas is much safer for children.

Mayra says:
I want to show what we can do, rather than what we cannot.

Children have a right to protection from all forms of violence, neglect, and abuse, but every year 40 million children are beaten so badly that they need medical care. Many street children become addicted to drugs to block out the misery of their lives. More than 1 million children in the world are imprisoned for begging, loitering, or living on the street. Very few are convicted of violent crimes. They are cruelly treated by police and authorities who ignore their legal rights and disregard the key objectives of juvenile justice—the child's rehabilitation and reintegration into society. Six countries have executed juvenile offenders during the last decade.

Hundreds of children walked in an Anti-Smacking March through London, UK, to the Prime Minister's residence.

"Children should be respected and treated with the same dignity as adults. Corporal punishment is shameful, insulting, humiliating, frightening, and painful. It has to stop, now!" **Boaz**, 15, Kenya, *World's Children's Ombudsman*

Hanwool Park, 17, South Korea

"Bullying became so bad that I tried to kill myself."

Hanwool makes videos about bullying in school.

"I've been slapped and hit without any reason. I have a scar on my face and my eyes were injured from being beaten. Someone stole my things and sold them. Bullies threw chairs at me and my backpack was thrown out of the window. They spread malicious rumors about me, talked behind my back, locked me in the class-room, and excluded me from activities," Hanwool says. "I told my parents, but they didn't take it seriously. I told the school, but they wanted to keep it quiet. The bullying became so bad that I tried to jump from the fourth floor of the school in front of the teachers but the police came and stopped me. After, I just stayed in my room in the dark in a state of panic. Now I am making videos to raise awareness of school bullying in the hope that others won't have to suffer in silence as I did for six years."

Experts say school violence and suicide have become more serious and frequent in South Korea, partly due to competitive school programs that only focus on academic achievements, rather than on well-rounded personality education. The huge pressure on young people to achieve academic success can mean they behave aggressively, targeting the weak and powerless in the group.

"I had three hours of sleep. I sleep from 2 a.m. until 5 a.m. I had two hours of study on my own, and go to school for classes from 9 a.m. until 5 p.m. Coming back home from school, have a meal, study by myself from 6 p.m. to 9 p.m., get a private lesson from 9 p.m. to 11 p.m., and study on my own again from 11 p.m. to 2 p.m." (**boy**, 14, South Korea)

Many parents force their children to study, denying them the right to play. South Korean students have some of the highest test scores in the world, but Korea also has one of the world's highest teen suicide rates.

"When children play, the world wins." Play is not a luxury; it is a tool for education and health. **Right To Play** uses sport and play to teach important life lessons and develop skills. It inspires and empowers youth to overcome the effects of poverty, conflict, and disease in disadvantaged communities to create a healthier and safer world. www.righttoplay.com

"One child exploited is one child too many."

Cheryl with child survivor at the PREDA Foundation in the Philippines.

"Can you imagine waking up, not in your comfortable bedroom, but locked in a damp, wooden shack with no windows or fresh air? Can you imagine not getting your weekly allowance to spend on candy and clothes, but being beaten and abused if you don't bring enough money home? Can you imagine that on a Saturday morning, instead of getting up to play video games, or getting ready to hang out with friends, you are forced to wake up and provide services for men? This is the reality for more than two million children exploited worldwide. And if circumstances were different...if you were born into a different family, into a different life, it could be you. Child slaves do not choose this reality," Cheryl says, "so this is why you should care about the exploitation of children."

In grade 10, after learning about the horrors of child sexual exploitation, Cheryl became angry and frustrated. She had a chance to travel to Sri Lanka and arranged to meet with exploited children there. When she asked them how she could help, they said, "Tell our stories." Back home, Cheryl and nine others founded OneChild, a non-profit organization that focuses on stopping the commercial exploitation of children and providing homes and counselling for survivors.

Cheryl says:

Every action that you take, good or bad, creates a ripple effect. But a good action can inspire someone else to do something good, and their action will inspire another...and another...and that's how positive change happens.

"Stop! Stop! Where are you going?" **Poonam Thapa** questions a man and young girl at a border station to make sure the girl isn't one of thousands of poor Nepalese girls who are lured into India by child traffickers each year to suffer the same fate as Poonam. When she was 14, Poonam was tricked and sold to a brothel in India where she was drugged and beaten before being rescued and taken to the Maiti Nepal rehabilitation center. Volunteers from the center work as borderguards to help prevent child trafficking, the illegal transportation across borders of children who are forced to become, sex workers, slave laborers, and child soldiers. The trading and selling of slaves is the most profitable criminal business in the world next to drugs and the arms trade.

Kids Take Action!

"*This world needs us. Our world suffers from the absence of social, economic, and political justice—where the strong dominate the weak. Youths from all cultures and nations are able to overcome political, religious, and cultural borders to help make this earth a better place, a more peaceful place, where people love and care about each other, and are treated equally.*" **Mahmoud Jabari** lived in Palestine, a place that shares a deeply painful history with neighboring Israel. After attending a Peace Camp to understand both sides of the conflict, Mahmoud founded Young Reporters Across Borders, to teach young people how to use journalism to listen and understand each other and exercise their right to say what they think.

"*Children in care often don't have a bike of their own, and I think that's wrong—we want to have fun like everyone else. My dream is for all children in care to have good lives, and have their rights respected just like other children.*" **David Pullin**, 15, of the UK, lived with a foster family after his alcoholic parents often left him hungry and alone. He joined Children's Voice, a forum where children in care can meet up and talk about what they've been through. David sits on a Children in Care Council to make sure children with a similar background are treated well.

"*Life in the refugee camp is very difficult and crowded. Sometimes children are denied schooling or food. Boys and girls were keeping their pain inside. Our radio broadcast, Children for Children, makes them feel less alone.*" **Baruani Ndume** was seven when his family was killed and he fled to a Tanzanian refugee camp to seek asylum. More than half of the world's refugees, an estimated 20 million, are children. They are exposed to dangers and may become separated from their families. Some spend their entire childhood in "temporary" displacement camps.

"*A single person, even if young and inexperienced, can become a catalyst for change. Young people are often told that they are 'leaders of tomorrow.' I urge young people to become leaders today.*" **Meghan Pasricha**, 16, USA, fought for the right to a healthy environment after years of struggling to breathe in smoke-filled public spaces. Meghan, a chronic asthma sufferer, founded the Anti-Tobacco Action Club at her school to educate youth and mobilize them to support tough indoor smoking bans.

"Hope is what keeps us going. It's what keeps us striving for the lives we deserve. I hope that my actions as an ability activist will leave the world more accepting and more accommodating for all people and not just people with disabilities, because we are all different and we all have the need to be accepted regardless of having a disability or not." **Chaeli Mycroft** of South Africa was born with Cerebral Palsy. At the age of 9, Chaeli, her sister Erin, and friends, Tarryn, Justine, and Chelsea Terry raised money for a motorized wheelchair. This project grew into the Chaeli Campaign, which helps children with disabilities obtain assistive equipment and treatment programs, and also defends their rights and acceptance. www.chaelicampaign.co.za

"Nothing for us, without us!"
Sandra Jimenez Loza, 13, of Mexico inspired more than three million children to express their opinions and exercise their rights as young citizens by voting in the UN Say Yes for Children campaign. In the media, she urged kids not to wait as spectators for other people to do what kids should do themselves. The children called for action on these ten priorities rated in order of importance:
1: Educate Every Child **2:** Leave No Child Out **3:** Fight Poverty
4: Care for Every Child **5:** Stop Harming and Exploiting Children
6: Fight HIV/AIDS **7:** Listen to Children **8:** Put Children First
9. Protect the Earth **10:** Protect Children from War.

"I wish to help children around the world get a birth certificate. Having a name and a nationality gives them the chance to lead a more fulfilling life and be saved from exploitation."
After getting her own registration, **Francia Simon**, of the Dominican Republic, helped many other "invisible" children obtain documents that help them access healthcare, school, a passport, a bank account, voting, and employment. Each year 51 billion births are not registered. In 2010, Francia, 16, was awarded The International Children's Peace Prize which is presented annually to a child whose actions have made a difference in countering problems affecting children around the world.

Kids Create!

"Open my school! I want to study and I am not afraid of anyone."
Malala Yousafzai, 11, Pakistan. When the Taliban forced their way into the Swat valley, they blasted hundreds of girls' schools. Afraid they might throw acid on her face or worse, Malala pretended to comply with the ban on educating girls by not wearing her school uniform and hiding books under her shawl. Malala courageously opposed the Taliban by writing an online diary of her experience and appeared on television.

A documentary, *A Schoolgirl's Odyssey*, chronicled Malala's journey into exile during the civil war, and her return to her school. In 2012, Malala was shot in the head by Taliban thugs. Miraculously, she survived to continue her activism.

"Young people should accept themselves for who they are."

Canadian **Scott Heggart**, 15, was attracted to all sports but Scott was also attracted to males. Feeling he would never be accepted by his teammates who used hateful homophobic words, Scott became depressed and lonely. He began to hate himself. When he shared his secret with his family members, they were understanding and supportive. Over the next year, Scott posted a YouTube video each day sharing his struggles about being a gay jock. He received support from more than 500,000 people around the world. When he finally came out to his teammates by changing his Facebook status to "in a relationship" and adding a photo of his boyfriend, Scott's inbox filled up with messages of respect, support, and apologies.

"I have a dream to see my mother again."

Kamran Safi, 13, left his home in Afghanistan after his life was threatened by the Taliban extremists who killed his father. Kamran traveled alone and in hiding for 3,554 miles (5,720 km), always in fear of being beaten or arrested in strange countries, until he was taken into care in England. He told his story in a short animated film, *Kamran's Journey*, which sheds light on the struggles facing millions of unaccompanied minors on the move. Many leave their homes for the chance of a job, education, or a better life; others to escape violence and abuse at home, an arranged marriage or other cultural practices, natural disasters, or wars. They are highly vulnerable to child labor, exploitation, and other abuses. Their numbers are expected to grow, especially with increasing climate change. (Kamran's film is part of Youth Producing Change: http://ff.hrw.org/film/youth-producing-change)

I've changed the behavior of my friends and others. The school is cleaner."

Shanta Chaudhary, 14, Nepal, chairs the Sanitation Club at her school. With drama and songs, club members teach their community about water safety, hygiene, and the need to construct toilets. Children pay the highest price in an unhygienic world where more than one billion people struggle without safe water and one in three lacks a toilet. Waterborne diarrhea kills a child every 15 seconds, and underlies much of the world's disease and malnutrition. www.unicef.org/wash

When I born, I black/ When I grow up, I black/ When I go in the sun, I black/ When I scared, I black/ When I sick, I black/ And when I die, I still black/ And you white fellow/ When you born, you pink/ When you grow up, you white/ When you go in sun, you red/ When you cold, you blue/ When you scared, you yellow/ When you sick, you green/ And when you die, you gray/ And you calling me colored?

Anonymous UK schoolchild.

I Think of You

I always say:/ "I don't like this soup!/ Can I throw it away?"/ Then I think of you,/ with nothing to eat!/ I always say:/ "This shirt is for girls!/ I want Kaka's jersey!/ Then I think of you,/ with only rags to wear!/ I always say:/ "I don't feel like doing my homework!/ I don't like going to school!"/ Then I think of you,/ forced to work!/ I always say:/ "Mom, can I go to the park/ to play with my friends?"/ Then I think of you,/ Sent off to war with a gun!/ I complain when my mom scolds me./ Then I think of you,/ abandoned./ I think of you!

Teseo, 11

Nina, 15, Poland

Children's Views of Child Labour is an exhibition that demonstrates the important role child artists can play in raising awareness of social injustices. The artists and poets, some of whom are former laborers, are showing solidarity with the millions of children who are deprived of their basic human rights. They call on decision-makers to eliminate child labor and to work to give all children an education.

What YOUth Can Do

Volunteer

"When we take responsibility to help others, nothing feels better or teaches us more about our own power and worth. Heroes don't start out as heroes—they end up there after following their passions." **Talia Leman**, USA, was 10 when she raised millions of dollars to help Hurricane Katrina survivors. She started RandomKid to give kids the resources to help children who can't help themselves. Talia believes that anyone is someone. Here is her advice on how to get started:

1. Take the first step. Small efforts have great power. Big outcomes are dependent on them.
2. Find an adult who will help and give you advice.
3. Be responsive to others. Be willing to change your plan. Try new and different things. Invite everyone in the team to lead with their talent.
4. If you meet a dead-end, head in a new direction. If you don't know the right way, trust that the path will rise to meet you.
5. Your youth will get attention. Your inexperience will lead to great things because you don't know what isn't possible.
6. Believe in yourself. You'll be amazed by what you can do.

Talia asked kids to Trick or Treat to help Hurricane Katrina victims.

Learn, Care, Share

"I wondered who had stolen their smiles and what we could do to help them."
Guo Yujie, 14, of China was deeply moved by her visit to children living in an HIV/AIDS village, realizing that they were just like her. Guo started a website, and spearheaded many activities in her school to inspire others to learn the facts, share knowledge with friends and family, and care for friends and families affected by HIV/AIDS.

Donate

"For my birthday party I asked for a donation so I could buy some mosquito nets so children will not get bit by mosquitoes when they sleep." **Kira**, 7, Canada

Every 30 seconds a child dies of malaria, the number one cause of death in children under five. Malaria is preventable but poor families cannot afford medicine or insecticide-treated bed nets. One $10 bed net protects three children from the mosquitoes that carry malaria.
www.spreadthenet.org

Raise awareness

The World Walks for Water campaign raises awareness among children about the importance of clean water and adequate sanitation in developing countries. Women and children walk 40 billion hours per year carrying water weighing 40 pounds (18 kg), which is still not safe to drink. It causes death, disease, missed education and missed lives.

Dutch children walk 3.7 miles (6 km), carrying heavy, water-filled backpacks on World Water Day to raise money to finance water projects.

Join an organization to help make a better world

"We are the first generation that can eradicate poverty." When **Hugh Evans** of Australia was 14, he saw destitute children scavenging through a garbage dump. He realized that it was pure chance that he lived in a safe and comfortable home with plenty of food to eat while others lived in poverty without even the basic elements of human dignity. This revelation led to his vision for the Oaktree Foundation, Australia's first youth-run aid organization with a mission of young people working together to end global poverty.

Hanif, 15, Indonesia

Speak out!

Those with more than enough are damaging our world blindly, while those with nothing suffer. We are late, but not too late. Trust me, the best time to act is now." **Mohamed Axam Maumoon**, 15, Maldives, spoke at the United Nations Climate Change Conference in Copenhagen on behalf of the 160 young people who drafted a declaration.

Take the 'It Gets Better' Pledge

Everyone deserves to be respected for who they are. I pledge to spread this message to my friends, family and neighbors. I'll speak up against hate and intolerance whenever I see it at school and at work. I'll provide hope for lesbian, gay, bi, transgendered and other bullied teens by letting them know that "It Gets Better."

Acknowledgments

For Louise,
and all the precious grandchildren of the world.

Acknowledgments
I extend my thanks and appreciation to all the activists included in this book. My sources for many of the stories came from organizations dedicated to honoring young rights activists. Special thanks to the International Children's Peace Prize,* UNICEF,** and all the foundations and individuals who sent photographs and drawings. Ndale's story, and the quotes from Poonam and David are from *The Globe*, the magazine of the World's Children's Prize.*** I am grateful for the financial support from the Ontario Arts Council Writers' Reserve and the Canada Council for the Arts. Thanks to my models, Sophia, Bianca, Avalene, Robin, and Morgan. Kudos to the Second Story team for their guidance and advice. Chris, my partner in work and life, was invaluable, as always.

* The International Children's Peace Prize is awarded annually to an exceptional child whose remarkable actions have improved their own situation and that of children in their environment and around the world. The prize provides a platform for children to express their ideas and personal involvement in children's rights. www.kidsrights.org To learn about all the winners go to www.childrenspeaceprize.org

** UNICEF: The United Nations Children's Fund was created to work with others to overcome the obstacles that poverty, violence, disease, and discrimination place in a child's path. It believes that nurturing and caring for children are the cornerstones of human progress. www.unicef.org

*** The World's Children's Prize is an educational and empowerment program open to all schools and children. It promotes a more humane world where the rights of the child are universally respected, and where every new generation grows to be humane global citizens. It is supported by 58,000 schools in 108 countries with 27 million students, many of whom have had their rights violated and have learned their rights for the first time. In their Global Vote, up to 71 million children decide who should be their Child Rights Hero. The prize money is used to help children toward a better life. www.worldschildrensprize.org

For more information:
The Convention on the Rights of the Child:
www2.ohchr.org/english/law/crc.htm
Craig Kielburger: **www.freethechildren.com**

Dylan Mahalingam: **www.lilmdgs.org**
UNMDG: **www.unicef.org/mdg**
Emanuel Bagual: **www.myrights-skip.org**
Shannen Koostachin: **www.shannensdream.ca**
Ta'Kaiya Blaney: **www.takaiyablaney.com**
Zach Bonner: **www.littleredwagonfoundation.com**
Cheryl Perera: **www.onechild.ca**
The Chaeli Campaign: **www.chaelicampaign.co.za**
Children's Views of Child Labor: **www.ilo.org**
Talia Leman: **www.randomkid.org**
World Walks for Water: **www.worldwalksforwater.org**
Hugh: **www.theoaktree.org**
Mohamed Axam Maumoon: **www.youtube.com/watch?v=zDKRJvVHJKk**

Credits

The Star Thrower is based on a story by Loren Eiseley
Gabriela: ©UNICEF/NYHQ2002-0148/Markisz
Brickyard child: ©Roberto Romano
Reverse poem by Lacey, UNICEF
Anita: ©UNICEF/India/2006
Peggy's quote: We Are Family Foundation
Thandiwe: Dennis Brouchard/ Kids Rights
Emanuel: courtesy of the Dynamic Teen Company
Dump scavengers: courtesy of ILO/M.Crozet
Shannen: courtesy of Charles Dobie
Ta'Kaiya: courtesy of Wanda Griffiths
Bangladesh child: ©Md. Tanvirul Islam
Nujood: AFP 2008/Khaled Fazaa
Teresa: ©UNICEF/NYHQ2007-1620/Markisz
Ndale: Gunilla Hamne/ World's Children's Prize
Red Hand Day: courtesy of HRC/The Red Hand Campaign
Mayra: courtesy of Kimberly Gomes/ Kids Rights
Stop smacking: Heritage Images
Hanwool: courtesy of International Child Rights Center, South Korea
Drawing: courtesy of International Child Rights Center, South Korea
Poonam: Tora Mårtens/World's Children's Prize
Mahmoud: courtesy of Seeds of Peace
Chaeli: courtesy of the Chaeli Campaign
Francia: courtesy of Roy Beusker/KidsRights
Malala: ©Stringer Pakistan / Reuters
Toilets: ©UNICEF EAPRO MGLA00575/Jim Holmes/Mongolia
Drawing: courtesy of ©GenevaWorld
Spiderman: courtesy of Talia Leman
Walking 4 Water: courtesy of Mark Tiele Westra/AKVO
Drawing: courtesy of ©GenevaWorld/ Hanif

Library and Archives Canada Cataloguing in Publication

Wilson, Janet, 1952-
Our rights : how kids are changing the world / written and illustrated by Janet Wilson.

ISBN 978-1-926920-95-5

1. Social reformers—Biography—Juvenile literature. 2. Human rights workers—Biography—Juvenile literature. 3. Civil rights workers—Biography—Juvenile literature. 4. Children's rights—Juvenile literature. I. Title.

HN19.W54 2013   j303.48'40922   C2012-907905-7

Second Story Press gratefully acknowledges the support of the Ontario Arts Council and the Canada Council for the Arts for our publishing program. We acknowledge the financial support of the Government of Canada through the Canada Book Fund.

Printed and bound in China

Published by
Second Story Press
20 Maud Street, Suite 401
Toronto, Ontario, Canada
M5V 2M5
www.secondstorypress.ca